Vᵈ de José Mª Caselles y Tarrats S.C

D1141327

WALTHAM FOREST LIBRARIES

904 000 00272575

REAL
TAPAS

SANTA MARIA # 65

- Chips de yuca 375
- Anchoas con pan con tomate 675
- Mojama de atún con cebolla tierna y aceite de oliva 675
- Cecina de león 775
- Ensalada de castañas y calabaza y queso feta 675
- "Raviolis" con apio y mantequilla de cacahuete en ensalada 775
- Empanadillas de setas y pato confitado 415
- Ancas de rana marinadas con salvia y gengibre 675
- Guiso de caracoles con tortilla japonesa 925
- Sushi de verduras con salvia y pepino 750
- Maki de aguacate 2500
- Maki de gamba y lechón rebozado 1100
- Sushi variado
- Huevos de codorniz escalfados con pisto y chistorra 450
- Alcachofas "bota" a la plancha 900
- Tartar de vedella guisadas con berenjenas 625
- salteado de vedella 675
- Truchas de río con acelga, champiñones y judías 625
- Bacalao con boniato integral con shitake, espárragos y cecina 575
- mangas de pato y encurtidos 775
- (...)
- manzana 875
- mangas de vedella 775
- hígado de pato con pera y pimienta sichuan 850
- Alitas de pollo tandori 475
- Surtido de quesos 675

* A partir de 5 comensales sólo se sirve menú degustación *

= Postres =

- Piña colada con chupa-chups 450
- Helado de caki, plumb-cake y toffe 675
- Manzana reineta con bizcocho de frutos secos y helado de chocolate 675
- Trufas de chocolate 375

REAL
TAPAS

FIONA DUNLOP

75 authentic recipes to share

Photography by Jan Baldwin

MITCHELL BEAZLEY

An Hachette UK Company
www.hachette.co.uk

First published in Great Britain in 2002 by Mitchell Beazley,
an imprint of Octopus Publishing Group Ltd, Endeavour
House, 189 Shaftesbury Avenue, London WC2H 8JY

www.octopusbooks.co.uk

This edition published 2013 by Octopus Publishing Group

Copyright © Octopus Publishing Group Ltd 2013
Text copyright © Fiona Dunlop 2002, 2013

Photographs © Jan Baldwin 2002, 2013

All rights reserved. No part of this book may be reproduced
or utilized in any form or by any means, electronic or
mechanical, including photocopying, recording, or by any
information storage and retrieval system, without the prior
written permission of the publisher.

While all reasonable care has been taken in the preparation
of this book, neither the publishers nor the author can
accept any liability for any consequences arising from
the use thereof, or the information contained herein.

ISBN 978 1 84533 802 2

A CIP record for this book is available
from the British Library

Publisher Alison Starling
Art Director Jonathan Christie
Designer The Oak Studio
Photographer Jan Baldwin
Recipe Translator Ana Sims
Project Editor Jo Wilson
Assistant Production Manager Lucy Carter
Indexer Diana LeCore
Commissioning Editor for original edition Becca Spry
Editors for original edition Jamie Ambrose, Hattie Ellis,
Georgina Atsiaris

Printed and bound in China

Waltham Forest Libraries

904 000 00272575	
Askews & Holts	05-Jul-2013
641.812 DUN	£9.99
3953679	3

CONTENTS

INTRODUCTION

In the last twenty years or so, tapas have conquered the world, radiating from their Hispanic source to tease the taste-buds of anyone in search of a generous snack to accompany a glass of wine. Yet such pan-national culinary clones are mere shadows of the real thing, which is only found in Spain itself. Racy flavours, high contrasts, generous doses of virgin olive oil, ultra-fresh ingredients, fearless use of offal and obsessive use of salt cod or cured ham – these are just some of the hallmarks of Spanish tapas.

Naturally enough, much tipsy speculation has taken place over the origins of tapas. The word *tapa* ('lid'), from *tapar* ('to cover'), allegedly refers to slices of cheese or ham used to cover glasses of sherry in the hot, insect-infested bars of Andalucía. From these prosaic beginnings, so the story goes, came the tradition of serving small portions of bar food free with a glass of beer, wine or sherry.

An alternative theory stems from the 13th century, when the Castilian King Alfonso X, surrendering to doctor's orders to recuperate from an illness, spent long days in bed, sipping small glasses of restorative wine accompanied by reduced portions of food. His recovery was so painless that there soon followed a royal decree ordering taverns to only serve wine if accompanied by a snack.

Yet another, more down-to-earth, theory equates tapas with the punctuations of the rural working day, tiding over appetites and boosting energy in a climate not always conducive to huge meals or hard labour. Pre- or post-*siesta*, grazing was the way to go for Spain's agricultural masses.

Whatever their starting point, tapas have moved on and are now inextricably linked to the Spanish way of life. They have generated the *tapeo* (tapas bar crawl), a unique, mobile institution that brings swarms of families out on to the streets, when the heat of the day has passed, to stroll, chat and stop for a drink and – naturally – a tapa or two. The continuity of

the habit is ensured by the presence of many generations, from grandpas to babies, while floors scattered with used napkins, cocktail sticks, olive stones, mussel shells and the odd errant anchovy all point clearly to the lip-smacking gusto of the activity. The *tapeo* is spontaneous, convivial and informal, it occurs within customary twice-a-day time-slots on a year-round basis. Ever different, the Basques opt for the word *poteo*, a derivative of *potes* ('pots' or 'jars'), from which wine or cider was once drunk.

Traditionally, each bar cooked up only one speciality, and this enforced peripatetic snacking on a population only too happy to

prolong its voluble socialising. Drunkenness is rare; while spirits and decibels soar, excess alcohol is rapidly absorbed by sporadic feeding. You still find one-off house specialities in smaller towns, but today's bars are more likely to chalk up a list of tapas and *raciones* (larger portions) of the day. Again, the exception comes from the Basque Country, where tapas are replaced by *pintxos* (or *pinchos*), finger snacks that resemble French canapés and that are scaling new heights of diversity and elaborateness.

All this was part of the late 20th century awakening and post-Franco bounce, when sophisticated *nueva cocina* (new cuisine)

galvanised chefs into producing ever-more inventive juxtapositions of ingredients and flavours. The initial impetus came from France via the Basques, and has since conquered local cuisine, from Seville to Barcelona, Madrid to Salamanca. This renaissance has inspired most of this book's recipes, which were created by chefs in search of exciting gastronomic departures. Glutinous bean stews and sad-looking *picadillo* (diced vegetable) salads, move on! There remain, too, the tapas classics, whose earthy flavours are unbeatable reflections of Spanish history, landscapes and produce, and which differ radically from region to region. Few tapas are universal in Spain; local produce is paramount. The 'rural-folkloric revival'

(a term coined by anthropologist T. Seppilli in 1992) is galloping ahead, highlighting local delicacies (anything from a black pudding, a pulse or an organic cured ham to a snail or a quail) that may even be produced in a specific valley or village. This is nurturing a taste for quality. One exception is the ubiquitous *ensaladilla* ('little salad' or Russian salad), a tapa of canned vegetables smothered in mayonnaise, that just won't go away. For foreigners bemused by its similarity to 1960s airline food, the *ensaladilla* raises questions. But then the French still snack on bland *croque monsieur*, so why not? Mayonnaise itself appears again and again, whether straight out of a jar or as garlic-enhanced *alioli*. But then it did start life in Mahón, Menorca, so who's to judge?

The gastronomic euphoria of the last few decades goes hand-in-hand with Spain's new-found identity and awareness of the outside world. These, in turn, have led Spaniards to a greater awareness of their own roots and cultural heritage. Regionalism is king and *Denominación de Origen Controllado*, or *DOC*, labels of regulated quality are proliferating; once used only for the country's wines, as *Denominación de Origen (DO)* or with the attached *Calificada (DOCa)* for Rioja, this type of quality control now extends to foodstuffs such as white beans or suckling pigs. Travelled chefs concoct fusion food harking back to Spain's complex cosmopolitan history.

The wheel turns full circle to reintegrate Arab contrasts of flavour and techniques that were originally brought to the country by the Moors. Similarly, the Roman art of fish preserving never went away. Jewish input over the centuries was huge, from *boquerones* (anchovies in vinegar) to *empanadas* (meat pies), and it is possible that tapas derived from Middle Eastern meze. The bass-line of most Spanish cuisine continues to be dominated by New World produce: the potato, tomato, broad bean and bell pepper. Add to this Phoenician, Greek and Jewish input and you come to realise that by tasting Spanish tapas, you taste a good part of the globe.

VERDURAS

VEGETABLES

ALCACHOFA CON ACEITE DE OLIVA NEGRA

ARTICHOKE HEARTS WITH BLACK OLIVE OIL

This ultra-simple recipe is light and delicious, yet it looks like a work of art.

Prepare the black olive oil by mixing the olives and oil in a blender until the olives are finely chopped.

Just before serving, place the artichoke hearts on a plate and pour the black olive oil all over them.

FOR 8 TAPAS

- - - - - - - - - - - - -

100g (3½oz) pitted black olives

200ml (7fl oz) extra virgin olive oil

8 artichoke hearts, cooked, or canned and
    well drained

ENSALADA DE CALABAZA,

PUMPKIN, CHESTNUT, FETA CHEESE AND POMEGRANATE SALAD

FOR 8 TAPAS

Leaves from half an oakleaf lettuce or 175g (6oz) lamb's lettuce, torn into bite-sized pieces

1 small curly endive (frisée) lettuce, coarse leaves removed and torn into bite-sized pieces

1 bunch watercress

225g (8oz) feta cheese, broken into small cubes

1½ spring onions, thinly sliced

seeds of 1 pomegranate

200g (7oz) chestnuts, cooked, peeled and halved

350g (12oz) pumpkin flesh, cut into fine julienne strips

2 tbsp white wine vinegar

6 tbsp extra virgin olive oil

salt and pepper to taste

The happy collusion between Asian influences and Catalonia's fantastic array of autumnal produce has inspired this salad tapa. Every autumn, chestnut-roasters take root in the streets of Spain, while market stalls acquire the Dali-esque shapes and colours of abundant squash varieties. In this recipe, you can vary or simplify the lettuce types, as the main interest lies in the balance of fresh pumpkin, chestnuts, feta and sweet pomegranate seeds.

Arrange all the salad ingredients in 8 individual bowls or 1 large one.

Make the vinaigrette by whisking the white wine vinegar and olive oil together and seasoning with the salt and pepper.

Dress the salad lightly, toss thoroughly, and serve immediately.

PUERROS CON VINAGRETA

LEEKS WITH A SUMMER VEGETABLE VINAIGRETTE

For centuries, leeks were relegated to support roles in Castilian cooking, but they are back on centre stage, particularly in the province of Segovia, where they are extensively cultivated. In this recipe, the colourful vegetable vinaigrette that covers the stacked white leeks makes for a particularly refreshing summer tapa.

FOR 6 TAPAS

12 slim leeks, white portion only, stripped of outer layer and root

salt to taste

1 tbsp olive oil

1 onion, finely chopped

1 small red pepper, finely chopped

1 small green pepper, finely chopped

100g (3½oz) gherkins, rinsed of vinegar and finely chopped

100g (3½oz) capers, rinsed of vinegar, brine or salt and finely chopped

2 small green tomatoes, finely chopped

125ml (4fl oz) extra virgin olive oil

2 tbsp white wine vinegar

1 bunch watercress

At least 1 hour before serving, cook the leeks in plenty of salted boiling water and 1 tbsp olive oil for about 12 minutes. Drain, cool the leeks and cut them in half lengthways.

Prepare the vegetable vinaigrette by mixing together the onion, peppers, gherkins, capers and tomatoes. Coat with the olive oil and wine vinegar. Season with salt to taste.

Just before serving, stack the leeks on a plate on a bed of watercress, and cover with the chopped vegetables.

PATATAS AL POBRE

POOR MAN´S POTATOES

There are endless variants to this recipe in southern Spain, some of which include red or green peppers. If you want to incorporate peppers, they should be seeded and sliced and added immediately after the onion and before the potatoes.

FOR 6 TAPAS

10 tbsp olive oil for frying

2 large Spanish onions, sliced into rings

6 medium-sized firm potatoes, peeled and sliced

salt to taste

1 tbsp sherry vinegar

3 cloves garlic, minced

In a heavy frying pan, heat 2 tbsp oil and fry the onions for 10 minutes, stirring occasionally, until they are golden.

Add the remaining oil, allow to heat, then add the potatoes and cook for a further 15–20 minutes, until they are tender. Season with salt and drain off any excess oil.

Mix the vinegar and garlic together, pour over the potatoes and then stir. Serve immediately.

ESPINACAS CON GARBANZOS A LA ANDALUZA

ANDALUCIAN-STYLE SPINACH WITH CHICKPEAS

This classic Andalucian dish has travelled to tapas bars all over Spain, such is its earthy appeal. The spinach and chickpeas are, surprisingly, Moorish imports.

FOR 6 TAPAS

1 kg (2lb 4oz) fresh spinach, washed, and destalked

50ml (2fl oz) olive oil

300g (10½oz) cooked chickpeas, drained

1 tsp ground cumin

salt and pepper to taste

3 cloves garlic

1 slice bread, fried in oil until golden

1 tsp red wine vinegar

2 tbsp water

1½ tsp sweet paprika

Cook the spinach in a covered pan, in the water that clings to it after washing, for about 4 minutes, until it is wilted. Let it cool, then press out the excess water. Chop roughly.

Sauté the spinach in the oil on a low heat for about a minute. Stir in the chickpeas, cumin, salt and pepper.

Pound the garlic and fried bread with a pestle and mortar or grind them in a blender until fine. Add to the spinach and mix well.

Add the vinegar, water and paprika, and cook over a low heat, stirring constantly, for about a minute. Serve at once in individual earthenware dishes.

PATATAS ALIÑADAS
SEASONED POTATO MASH

This is a delicious tapa created from the simplest ingredients. Seasoned mash is generously bathed in extra virgin olive oil from Andalucía, often premier oils from Baena or Priego de Cordoba (mixing Hojiblanca and Picudo varieties). Don't worry if you can't get hold of this oil, but do use the best you can find with a grassy flavour.

FOR 6 TAPAS

1 kg (2¼lb) new potatoes, scrubbed

3 spring onions, white part only, finely chopped

3 green peppers, finely chopped

9 tbsp extra virgin olive oil, preferably from a single estate

3 tbsp white wine vinegar

salt and pepper

few sprigs flat-leaf parsley

Cook the potatoes in boiling salted water for about 20 minutes, or until they are cooked.

Remove the skins and mash the potatoes, then push the mash through a sieve or potato ricer. Add the finely chopped onions and peppers.

Slowly add the oil and vinegar, beating until the mash is thick and creamy. (If more is necessary, add in proportions of 3 oil to 1 vinegar.)

Season with salt and pepper and serve immediately, mounded on to small individual plates with a few sprigs flat-leaf parsley.

PATATAS A LA IMPORTANCIA
POTATOES OF GREAT IMPORTANCE

Another of Spain's sustaining 'peasant' snacks, this dish is made from basic ingredients with strong flavours.

FOR 4 TAPAS

2 large potatoes, peeled and cut in 1-cm (½-inch) slices

100g (3½oz) cooked ham, in thin slices

100g (3½oz) French Chaumes or Port Salut cheese, in thin slices

salt to taste

beaten egg for coating

flour for coating

250ml (9fl oz) olive oil for frying

FOR THE SAUCE

2 tbsp olive oil

7 cloves garlic, thinly sliced

1 bunch flat-leaf parsley, chopped

2 tbsp flour

250ml (9fl oz) white wine

Between each 2 potato slices, place 1 slice of ham and 1 slice of cheese. Season with salt. Dip in beaten egg, then flour, and fry in hot oil until the potato is golden and cooked. Remove.

To make the sauce, heat the oil in a frying pan. Add the garlic and sauté until tender. Add the parsley and stir. Blend in the flour, stirring until the mixture has thickened. Take the pan off the heat and stir constantly while adding the wine a little at a time.

When the wine is incorporated, put the pan back on the heat and bring to the boil, stirring. Simmer for 5 minutes. Pour the sauce over the potatoes and serve immediately.

FRITURA DE LA HUERTA
FRITTATA OF GARDEN VEGETABLES

The choice of vegetables is yours but, as always, follow the seasons for the best results; obvious alternatives to those in this recipe are green and red peppers. The light batter produces a crisp coating that resembles tempura.

FOR 4 TAPAS

40g (1½oz) onion, cut into thin rings

25g (1oz) flour

55g (2oz) cauliflower, separated into florets and briefly cooked

1 egg, beaten

55g (2oz) dry breadcrumbs

55g (2oz) aubergine, peeled and cut into small cubes

1 tbsp milk

olive oil for frying

salt to taste

Dip the onion rings in flour. Dip the cauliflower first in flour, then in egg, then in breadcrumbs. Moisten the aubergine cubes in milk and then coat with flour.

Heat about 6cm (2½ inches) olive oil in a pan and, when hot, cook the vegetables seperately. Drain immediately on paper towels and then sprinkle with salt.

Arrange attractively on a plate and serve at once.

AJO BLANCO
CHILLED ALMOND SOUP

This soup, invented by the Moors to counteract Andalucía's baking hot summers, can look divinely minimalist served in white bowls afloat with muscatel grapes. It makes a refreshing change from some of Andalucía's stronger flavours, as the almond is extremely subtle.

FOR 4 TAPAS

- - - - - - - - - - - -

250g (9oz) blanched almonds

3 cloves garlic

85g (3oz) white breadcrumbs

500ml (18fl oz) water

2 tbsp sherry vinegar

salt to taste

6 tbsp olive oil

8 Muscatel (or similar) grapes

extra virgin olive oil to serve

Finely grind the almonds and garlic in a blender. Add the breadcrumbs, water, vinegar and salt and blend for 2 minutes until smooth.

Slowly add the olive oil, while continuing to blend, until you have a creamy liquid. Refrigerate for at least 1 hour.

Serve in individual soup bowls, with a grape or two and a light drizzle of extra virgin olive oil in each one.

PISTO CON HUEVO DE CODORNIZ
RATATOUILLE WITH QUAIL'S EGG

Pisto originated in La Mancha, but soon conquered the south and became Andalucía's answer to Provençal ratatouille – a mixture of braised Mediterranean vegetables – served with a fried egg. When preparing the vegetables, keep them in separate dishes so that you can easily add them successively.

FOR 4 TAPAS

6 green peppers, diced

1 large onion, diced

olive oil

500g (1lb 2oz) aubergine, peeled and diced

500g (1lb 2oz) courgette, diced

500g (1lb 2oz) tomatoes, diced

salt and pepper to taste

4 quail's eggs

In a large pan, sauté the peppers and onion in about 2 tbsp olive oil until they are softened. Add the aubergine and sauté for 5 more minutes. Add the courgette and sauté for 3 more minutes. You may need more oil.

Add the tomatoes, lower the heat, and simmer the vegetables together for 20 minutes. Season 5 minutes before the cooking time has ended.

Quickly fry the quail's eggs in a little olive oil.

To serve, heap generous portions of ratatouille on to individual serving plates and top with a fried egg.

CHAMPIÑONES EN SALSA VERDE

MUSHROOMS IN PARSLEY SAUCE

Serve this tapa in a shallow terracotta dish to show off the juicy mushrooms and their green sauce. This dish is quite delicious and the ingredients are available all year round.

FOR 8 TAPAS

100ml (3½fl oz) virgin olive oil

6 cloves garlic, minced

½ red chilli pepper or 2 dried cayenne peppers

1kg (2¼lb) fresh, white mushrooms, cleaned and halved or quartered, depending on their size

salt and pepper to taste

1 tbsp flour

FOR THE SAUCE

2 cloves garlic, minced

leaves from a large bunch of flat-leaf parsley, finely chopped

200ml (7fl oz) white wine

salt and pepper to taste

First, make the sauce, mix the garlic, parsley, white wine, salt and pepper for the sauce in a blender and set aside.

Pour the olive oil into a casserole, add the garlic and cook gently until tender. Add the chilli pepper and mushrooms and increase the heat. Cook, stirring constantly, until the juice has been drawn out of the mushrooms. Season and continue to simmer over a moderately high heat for about 10 minutes, stirring occasionally, until the juice has evaporated.

Sprinkle the flour over the mushrooms and stir to blend well. Remove the pan from the heat and slowly add the sauce ingredients, making sure you incorporate them well. Return the pan to the heat and bring to the boil, stirring all the time. Simmer for 5 minutes, until you have a fairly thick sauce; add a little water if you want to thin it down. Serve hot.

HUEVOS Y QUESOS

EGGS & CHEESES

TORTILLA DE PATATAS
POTATO TORTILLA WITH WHISKY SAUCE

FOR 6 TAPAS

100ml (3½fl oz) olive oil

1 kg (2¼lb) potatoes, peeled and cubed

3 eggs, beaten

salt and pepper to taste

FOR THE WHISKY SAUCE (SALSA DE WHISKY)

3 cloves garlic, finely sliced

2 tbsp olive oil

15g (½oz) butter

1 tbsp lemon juice

1 tbsp whisky

2 tbsp strong beef stock

There are hundreds of variants of tortilla across every region of Spain, but the tortilla *de patatas* is a real Spanish classic. This Sevillian version comes doused in a whisky sauce.

Heat the olive oil in a frying pan. Cook the potatoes in the oil over a very low heat for about 15 minutes, until they are tender but not brown.

Meanwhile, make the sauce. Sauté the garlic slices in the olive oil until they are tender. Add the butter, lemon juice, whisky and beef stock. Cook over a low heat, stirring occasionally, for 15 minutes, until reduced.

In a bowl, mix the potatoes with the beaten eggs and season to taste. Pour the mixture back into the frying pan and cook over a low heat for 3-4 minutes. When the tortilla is firm but not dry, cover the frying pan with a plate of equal size and, grasping the plate and pan, turn the tortilla out on to the plate.

Carefully slide the tortilla back into the pan and cook for another 3 minutes to brown the other side.

Turn out on to a serving plate and cool for at least 5 minutes. Slices can be served hot or at room temperature with the whisky sauce. Garnish with a whole pickled garlic clove, and herbs such as snipped chives and chopped parsley.

TORTILLA CACHONDA
TRICKY TORTILLA

You hardly know this is an omelette, albeit Spanish-style, because it is covered in a deliciously thick layer of creamy alioli – hence the dish's name. Cut a slice, however, and you know you're in the realm of tortilla. If you have a small frying-pan, so much the better to make individual tortillas, but this dish also works when made as one large tortilla.

FOR 4 TAPAS
- - - - - - - - - - - -

olive oil for frying

100g (3½oz) chorizo or other spicy cured
    sausage, thinly sliced

2 medium potatoes, cooked, peeled
    and sliced

½ small onion, finely chopped and sautéed
    until soft

3 eggs, beaten

salt and pepper to taste

FOR THE ALIOLI

2 cloves garlic

sea salt

1 egg yolk

125ml (4fl oz) olive oil

lemon juice to taste

salt and white pepper to taste

Make the alioli by crushing the garlic with a little sea salt. Stir the egg yolk into this and beat. Add the olive oil a drop at a time, continuing to beat and increasing the stream of oil as more becomes incorporated. You should end up with a thick, creamy mixture. When you've added all the oil, add the lemon juice, salt and pepper to taste. Cover and refrigerate immediately.

To make the tortilla, heat 1 tbsp olive oil in a small frying pan and sauté the chorizo quickly until just browned. Add the potatoes and onion and stir to brown.

Tip this mixture from the pan into a bowl, allow to cool a little, then stir in the eggs. Put 2 tbsp oil into the pan and pour the mixture back into it. Cook over a low heat for 3 minutes. When the omelette is firm but not dry, cover the frying pan with a flat plate and flip to turn the omelette out on to the plate. Slide the omelette back into the pan and cook for 3 minutes, to brown the other side. Cool for 5 minutes, then serve with a layer of alioli.

BERENJENA CON QUESO
AUBERGINE AND CHEESE FRITTERS

This, Casa Pali's flagship tapa, is easy and quick to prepare. It can even be half-cooked in advance and re-fried at the last minute. Your guests will need small knives and forks to devour it. For extra flavour, you can drizzle some liquid honey over the aubergines before serving.

FOR 4 TAPAS
----

4 thin slices of tangy, easy-to-melt cheese, such as French Chaumes, cut to fit the aubergine

8 thin slices of aubergine

salt to taste

2 beaten eggs for coating

flour for coating

olive oil for frying

For each tapa, place 1 slice of cheese between 2 slices of aubergine.

Season each sandwich of aubergine with salt, then dip it in egg and then flour. Fry in a little olive oil over a medium heat until golden on both sides. Serve hot.

PUERROS CON CREMA DE QUESO
CREAM CHEESE AND LEEK TOASTS

The traditional Castilian leek is dominant in this tapa, and perfectly complemented by the cream cheese.

FOR 4 TAPAS

75g (2¾oz) cream cheese

4 tbsp sunflower oil

20ml (¾fl oz) milk

2 slices white bread, crusts removed and cut in half

4 very fine leeks, cut in half lengthways, cooked and cooled

8 capers

Mix the cheese, oil and milk in a blender until creamy.

Toast the bread and place 2 leek halves on each piece.

Cover with the cheese sauce and garnish with a caper at each end.

Place under the grill for 1 minute. Serve hot.

TORTILLA DE AJETES, HABITAS Y JAMÓN
YOUNG GARLIC, BROAD BEAN AND HAM OMELETTE

This is a another flavoursome twist on the classic Spanish potato tortilla, and should be served at room temperature.

FOR 4 TAPAS

50g (1¾oz) tender young garlic, minced

olive oil for frying

50g (1¾oz) small young broad beans, cooked

40g (1½oz) serrano ham, cut into thin strips

3 eggs, well beaten

salt and pepper to taste

In a medium-sized frying pan, sauté the garlic in a little olive oil until soft and golden. Add the beans and ham strips and stir until warm.

Tip in the beaten eggs and seasoning and cook for 3-4 minutes, to form a firm but juicy omelette. Cool to room temperature, cut into triangular slices or squares and serve.

QUESO DE CABRA FRITO CON MIEL
FRIED GOAT'S CHEESE WITH HONEY

This is an exquisite, though rich, *nueva cocina* tapa. The hot goat's cheese is a delicious match for the cold caramelised onions. The honey should not be too highly flavoured, as this would drown the more subtle cheese, and it must be liquid so that it drizzles easily. The parsley is optional, but adds a splash of colour to this minimalist plate.

FOR 4 TAPAS

----

3 medium sweet red onions, very finely sliced

olive oil for frying

50g (1¾oz) sugar

150g (5½oz) cylindrical goat's cheese

1 egg, beaten

flour

2 tbsp liquid honey

1 tbsp finely chopped parsley

2 chive stalks

Prepare the garnish several hours before serving. Fry the onions in 3 tbsp oil over a low heat until they are really soft – it will take about 20 minutes. Drain off the excess oil and add the sugar. Stir until the sugar and onion are blended and the sugar has caramelised (about 8 minutes). Cool and refrigerate.

About 30 minutes before serving, form four perfect equal-sized balls of goat's cheese. Dip in the egg and then flour and fry in just enough oil to cover the bottom of the pan – turning carefully to lightly brown all sides. Drain on a paper towel.

Put the caramelised onions in the centre of a serving plate, and evenly space the fried cheese balls around it. Drizzle with honey, then sprinkle parsley over the top and add a criss-cross of chives. Serve at once.

QUESO CON MEMBRILLO
CHEESE AND QUINCE

Saltiness and sweetness combine
in this traditional Spanish tapa. You
could experiment with different
cheeses from the mountains of
Asturias, source of dozens of types
mixing cow, ewe and goat milk,
but ultimately little can beat the
satisfying tanginess of an extra
mature Manchego.

FOR 6 TAPAS

6 slices extra mature Manchego cheese

3 slices country bread

quince paste

dried fruit, flaked almonds and toasted pine
   nuts, to serve

Lay a piece of Manchego cheese on a half-slice
of country bread.

Place a smaller wedge of quince paste on top of
the cheese. Serve on a board with the dried
fruits and seeds.

CARNES

MEATS

FOIE GRAS, COURGETTE AND BITTER ORANGE TOASTS

This is an unusual combination of flavours, yet the end result is a wonderfully rich and luxurious tapa. Foie mi-cuit is a superior version of foie gras with a more subtle flavour, but if you can't get hold of it, use foie gras instead.

For each tapa, sandwich a quarter of the foie gras between 2 courgette slices. Brush with a little oil and grill for 3 minutes on each side.

Toast the bread, spread a little marmalade on each slice, and top with a courgette and foie gras sandwich. Dust with pepper and serve at once.

FOR 4 TAPAS

20g (¾oz) foie gras
8 × 3-mm (⅛-inch) courgette slices
olive oil
4 slices French bread, cut on the diagonal
1 tbsp best bitter orange marmalade
black pepper to taste

MUSLOS DE POLLO A LA MIEL

HONEY-BAKED CHICKEN THIGHS

This simple though beguiling recipe is dominated by the sweet honey, a Moorish legacy. Enjoy it in summer with dry white wine or bone-dry *fino*.

To prepare the honey sauce, combine all the ingredients except for the chicken thighs in a saucepan. Mix well and bring to a boil. Reserve.

Place the chicken thighs in a roasting tin, pour over the sauce and bake in a preheated oven and 180°C (350°F) Gas mark 4 for about 35 minutes, or until the chicken is dark and glossy and cooked through. Serve immediately.

FOR 4 TAPAS

- - - - - - - - - - -

250g (9oz) liquid honey

100g (3½oz) butter

1 tsp curry powder

1½ tsp dry mustard powder

75ml (2½fl oz) tomato ketchup

8 chicken thighs

HABITAS CON JAMÓN EN CONCHA DE ACHICORIA

IBERIAN HAM AND BROAD BEAN SALAD

Pulses are big in central Spain, but this recipe has chosen to limit their quantity while emphasising their visual appeal.

If using fresh broad beans, cook them in a little water for anything from 2–5 minutes, until tender (the younger they are the less cooking time they need). If using dried broad beans, soak them overnight, then cover them with fresh water and cook for 1–1½ hours, until tender. In both cases, once the beans have been drained and cooled slip them out of their skins.

Place the radicchio leaf in a container of iced water for about 15 minutes, until it brightens and stiffens.

Pour a little oil into a medium-sized frying pan. Add the garlic and cook slowly over a low heat until just golden. Add the ham strips, heat for 10 seconds, then add the broad beans. Season with salt to taste. Cook, stirring occasionally, until the beans are hot.

While the beans are frying, remove the radicchio leaf from the iced water, pat it dry and place it on a serving plate. Fill the leaf with the beans, allowing some to overflow on to the plate. Sprinkle with parsley and serve.

FOR 4 TAPAS

200g (7oz) fresh broad beans or 150g (5oz) dried broad beans

1 large, very fresh radicchio leaf

olive oil for frying

2 cloves garlic, finely sliced

100g (3½oz) Iberian or serrano ham, thickly sliced and cut into thin strips

salt to taste

2 tsp finely chopped parsley

GARBANZOS CON BUTIFARRA NEGRA

CHICKPEAS WITH BLACK PUDDING IN GARLIC AND PARSLEY

This classic Catalan tapa is the result of a wonderful blend of creamy chickpeas, sweet sultanas, meaty black pudding and crunchy pine nuts; a truly Hispanic assault on the senses!

Put 2 tbsp olive oil in a saucepan over a low heat, then sauté the onion until it is just tender. Add the garlic, parsley, sultanas and pine nuts and mix.

Add the black pudding and chickpeas and heat through, stirring all the time. Season with salt and pepper. Transfer to a serving platter, drizzle with olive oil and serve at once.

FOR 4 TAPAS

- olive oil
- ½ large onion, thinly sliced
- 1 clove garlic, finely chopped
- 2 tbsp finely chopped fresh parsley
- 25g (1oz) sultanas, soaked in hot water for 15 minutes and drained
- 10g (¼oz) pine nuts
- 150g (5½oz) black pudding, fried and coarsely chopped
- 1 × 400g can cooked chickpeas, drained and rinsed
- salt and pepper to taste

HIGADO DE PATO CON PERA Y PIMIENTO SZECHUAN

DUCK'S LIVER WITH SWEET PEARS AND SZECHUAN PEPPER

Duck's liver is the creamiest, smoothest liver you can get. Here it is perfectly combined with fresh poached pear and a hint of mild Szechuan pepper – although you can use chicken's liver if duck's liver isn't available. This is a rich tapa so you won't need second helpings.

FOR 4 TAPAS

60g (2¼oz) sugar

5 tbsp water

2 pears, peeled and thinly sliced

150g (5½oz) duck's liver, cut into 4 slices

1 tbsp olive oil

4 tsp Szechuan pepper

Mix the sugar and water in a pan and heat until the sugar has dissolved. Add the pears and poach until it is just tender. Drain the pears, reserving the liquid, and set the fruit aside. Bring the liquid to the boil and boil until syrupy. Return the pears to the liquid and mix well.

Sauté the liver in the oil until it is lightly browned on each side. Arrange on a plate.

Spoon some pear and syrup beside each liver slice. Grind the pepper and alongside. Serve immediately.

TENTEMPIÉ TRADICIONAL SEGOVIANO CON PATATAS NUEVAS

TRADITIONAL SEGOVIAN PORK AND POTATO 'FRY-UP'

This hearty Segovian dish has strong rural and wintry overtones straight from the heart of Old Castile. It traditionally filled empty peasant stomachs with an artful combination of left-over pork and seasonal new potatoes. Quick to prepare, it is more than just a substantial tapa, as it works equally well for brunch or as an evening snack.

FOR 6 TAPAS

500g (1lb 2oz) new potatoes, peeled and thinly sliced

1 large onion, thinly sliced

olive oil for frying

4 eggs

1 × 100g (3½oz) piece of roast pork, cut into strips about 1-cm (½-inch) wide

salt and pepper to taste

4 slices of fried French bread

Fry the potatoes and onion in plenty of olive oil over a low heat for about 20 minutes. They should be just cooked. Drain the excess oil from the frying pan and continue to brown the vegetables lightly.

Break the eggs directly over the potatoes and onions. Add the pork, season well, and stir to mix all the ingredients together. Cook until the eggs are just set. Serve immediately, accompanied by the fried bread.

ESPÁRRAGOS CON JAMÓN DE YORK Y QUESO

FRIED ASPARAGUS, HAM AND CHEESE BUNDLES

The classic marriage of ham and cheese is made more interesting by the texture and subtle flavour of the asparagus. Riojans love tinned asparagus spears so, for authenticity's sake, you needn't worry about finding the fresh variety – but use it if you prefer the extra crunch. This is one of Logroño's rare tapas that needs a knife and fork.

FOR 4 TAPAS

4 thin slices mild, easy to melt cheese, such as French Port Salut

4 asparagus spears, cooked *al dente*

4 thin slices cooked ham

beaten egg for coating

flour for coating

olive oil for frying

Place 1 slice of the mild cheese and 1 asparagus spear on each slice of cooked ham and carefully roll each one up to form a cylinder.

Dip the ham rolls in the egg and then the flour, then fry them in a little hot oil until they are golden brown. Serve immediately.

RED PEPPERS STUFFED WITH BLACK PUDDING

Spain offers endless varieties of black pudding, but other countries are less inventive, so find the best you can. The combination of the dark blood sausage and the fresh red pepper is quintessentially Spanish. Adding basil, ginger and pine nuts raises this classic dish to new heights.

FOR 8 TAPAS

8 small red peppers (preferably *piquillo*, can be canned) or 4 regular red peppers

olive oil

200g (7oz) black pudding (preferably from León)

1 egg, beaten

2 leaves fresh basil, finely chopped

25g (1oz) butter

2 tbsp flour

150ml (¼ pint) milk

75g (2¾oz) chickpeas, cooked and drained

½ tsp ground ginger

salt and pepper to taste

15g (½oz) pine nuts

If you are using canned *piquillo* peppers, just drain and halve them. If you are using raw peppers, brush them with olive oil and grill them until tender and partly black and blistered. Leave them aside until cool enough to handle, then peel off the skins, halve and seed them and set aside.

Fry the black pudding in an ungreased frying pan, breaking it into small pieces with a wooden spoon as you cook it. Remove from the heat, add the egg and stir until the egg has set. Add the basil and stir. Set aside.

Melt the butter, add the flour and stir to form a roux. Cook for 2 minutes. Remove from the heat and slowly add the milk, beating well. Bring back to the boil, stirring, until the sauce has thickened. Purée the chickpeas and add to the sauce. Add the ginger and seasoning. Simmer for 4 minutes. Pour into a shallow oven-proof dish.

Fill the pepper halves with the black pudding mixture, arrange them on the chickpea sauce and sprinkle with pine nuts. Cook at 180°C (350°F) Gas mark 4 for 10 minutes and serve.

CROQUETAS DE JAMÓN

HAM CROQUETTES

Competition in the ham croquettes stakes is ruthless. All over Spain, some sad attempts and a few delectable ones are created. The Casa Pali version is a rare bird, as it achieves the perfect blend of reassuring creaminess and smoky ham flavour in a deliciously crisp outer coating.

FOR 6 TAPAS

50g (1¾oz) butter

175g (6oz) flour

400ml (14fl oz) milk

1 small onion, finely chopped

1 tbsp olive oil

50g (1¾oz) Serrano ham, finely chopped

salt and pepper

2 beaten eggs for coating

fine, dry breadcrumbs for coating

100ml (3½fl oz) olive oil for frying

Melt the butter in a frying pan. Add the flour and stir for 3–4 minutes, until well blended, to form a roux. Take the pan off the heat and add the milk slowly, incorporating each addition into the roux and mixing until it is smooth before adding any more. Put the pan back on the heat and bring the milk up to the boil, stirring continually. The mixture should become very thick. Turn the heat down low and cook for about 5 minutes, stirring from time to time.

Gently sauté the onion in the olive oil until it is soft but not coloured. Add the pieces of ham.

Stir the onion and ham into the white sauce and season well with salt and pepper. Spread the mixture in a lightly greased pan to about 2cm (1 inch) thickness. Put in the fridge and chill for at least 2 hours.

When cool, cut the chilled mixture into small bars, then use your hands to shape each bar into a little cylinder.

Coat each croquette with egg and breadcrumbs. Pour about 8cm (3 inches) of olive oil into a pan and heat. Fry the croquettes a few at a time, until they are dark gold on the outside and warm and cooked in the middle. It's a good idea to test one to check whether your oil is at the optimum temperature; you don't want to brown the outside too much without also penetrating through to the middle of the croquette. Drain on kitchen paper and either serve hot or at room temperature.

JAMÓN, ALCACHOFA Y HABITAS CON ALI OLI

HAM, ARTICHOKE, BROAD BEAN AND ALIOLI TOASTS

This tapa and the following can be made together, offering alternative flavours but sharing the alioli topping. They are both simple to prepare, and the visual disguise of alioli leaves the ingredients as a surprise.

FOR 4 TAPAS

4 slices French bread, cut on the diagonal

100g (3½oz) Serrano ham

12 broad beans, cooked and drained

1 artichoke heart, cooked, drained, and sliced in 4

125g (4oz) alioli (see page 29)

paprika

Toast the bread and on each slice place a quarter of the ham, folded to fit the bread, 3 broad beans and a slice of artichoke heart.

Cover each tapa with a generous amount of alioli and dust with paprika before placing under a very hot grill for 15–20 seconds.

JAMÓN, SALMÓN, HABITAS CON ALIOLI Y QUESO

HAM, BROAD BEAN, SMOKED SALMON AND ALIOLI TOASTS

Ham and smoked salmon work well together here, united by the alioli disguise. Although not from Spanish waters, salmon has conquered Spanish palates in recent years.

FOR 4 TAPAS

4 slices white bread

1 slice cooked ham

12 broad beans, cooked and drained

125ml (4fl oz) alioli (see page 29)

1 slice of smoked salmon, chopped

Toast the bread and on each slice place a quarter of the ham, folded to fit the bread, and 3 broad beans.

Cover each tapa with a generous amount of alioli, then garnish with a little smoked salmon at each end before placing under a hot grill for 15–20 seconds.

CALDERETA DE CORDERO
LAMB STEW

This dish reflects the fact that lamb is still king in many parts of northern Spain. The stew could easily be served as a main dish if the quantity were increased and potatoes served alongside it. Note the mixture of lamb cuts adds to the flavour and texture.

FOR 6 TAPAS

2 tbsp olive oil

700g (1lb 9oz) lamb, ½ leg and ½ shoulder, cut into chunks

seasoned flour for coating

1 large onion, coarsely chopped

1 red and 1 green pepper, seeded and coarsely chopped

4 cloves garlic, chopped

½ red chilli pepper, seeded and chopped

1½ tsp hot smoked Spanish paprika (*pimentón de la Vera*)

1 tsp fresh thyme

1 tsp fresh rosemary

1 bay leaf

400ml (14fl oz) dry white wine

salt and pepper to taste

Heat the olive oil in a casserole. Dip the lamb chunks in flour, then brown them on all sides in the hot olive oil. Remove the lamb with a slotted spoon.

Put the onion, peppers, garlic and chilli in the casserole and cook in the same oil until tender.

Stir in the paprika, then add the lamb, herbs and white wine. Season and bring to the boil. Immediately turn the heat down very low, cover the pan, and cook the lamb gently for 1–1¼ hours, or until the meat is cooked through and very tender. Serve in a shallow earthenware dish.

ALBÓNDIGAS DE CORDERO A LA HIERBABUENA

MINTED LAMB MEATBALLS

Although Spain offers numerous variants on the meatball theme, these are arguably some of the tastiest in the entire country.

FOR 6 TAPAS

500g (1lb 2oz) lamb, minced

salt and pepper to taste

3 cloves garlic, minced

3 tbsp chopped fresh mint

2 small eggs, beaten

4 tbsp soft breadcrumbs

100ml (3½fl oz) dry sherry

1 tbsp olive oil for sautéing

FOR THE SAUCE

2 onions, finely chopped

1 clove garlic, finely chopped

1 tbsp olive oil for sautéing

225ml (8fl oz) thick tomato passata

1 tbsp dry sherry

water to thin, if needed

Combine all the meatball ingredients except for the olive oil in a large bowl and mix well. Form the meat into 2.5-cm (1-inch) diameter balls and sauté in oil until lightly browned on all sides. Drain on paper towels and set aside.

In the same pan, sauté the onions and garlic for the sauce in olive oil until soft. Add the tomato passata and sherry and simmer for 10 minutes. Remove from the heat.

In a blender, purée the sauce until smooth, adding a little water if it's too thick. Return the sauce to the sauté pan and add the meatballs. Bring to the boil and cook over a medium heat for about 10 minutes. Serve hot.

CHORIZO AL VINO

SPICY SAUSAGE IN RED WINE

In the north of Spain, chorizo is often cooked in cider, but this recipe uses red wine instead to create a warmer dish. It makes an excellent wintry tapa to accompany a couple of glasses of good Rioja.

FOR 4 TAPAS

550g (1¼lb) semi-cured chorizo or other spicy sausage

350ml (12fl oz) dry red wine

1 bay leaf

Place the sausage in a frying pan with the wine and bay leaf. Cover and cook over a low heat for 10–15 minutes, or until the wine has slightly reduced.

Remove the sausage from the pan and cut it into 1-cm (½-inch) slices. Return the slices to the wine and stir. Serve in individual earthenware dishes with chunks of French bread.

BISTEC TARTAR DE MICHELE
SPICY STEAK TARTARE

The palate is under a happy assault from this spicy tapa, with its onion, chilli peppers, capers and Tabasco.

FOR 6 TAPAS

- - - - - - - - - - - - -

4 tbsp finely chopped parsley

4 mild chilli peppers, seeded and finely chopped

1 small onion, finely chopped

50g (1¾oz) capers, rinsed of vinegar, brine or salt

500g (1lb 2oz) sirloin steak, minced

6 drops Tabasco sauce

salt and pepper to taste

extra virgin olive oil to taste

60g (2¼oz) Dijon herb mustard

In a bowl, mix together the parsley, chilli peppers, onion and capers. Add the minced sirloin and mix well.

Sprinkle with Tabasco, salt, pepper and oil to taste and mix to combine all the ingredients. Mound on a platter or on individual plates and serve with the herb mustard.

PINCHOS MORUNOS
SPICY PORK KEBABS

The name of these popular meat kebabs, '*morunos*', means 'Moorish'. Use good-quality pork (which during the Inquisition became Spain's most politically correct meat as it proved you were neither Muslim nor Jew), preferably organic, in order to make tender, highly-flavoured kebabs. They are ideally cooked on a barbecue, but taste fine cooked on a standard grill.

FOR 4 TAPAS

- - - - - - - - - - - -

3 tbsp olive oil

2 tbsp white wine vinegar

¼ tsp ground cumin

¼ tsp sweet Spanish paprika

¼ tsp hot Spanish paprika

2 tbsp chopped parsley

2 cloves garlic, minced

500g (1lb 2oz) lean pork, cut in
　　2.5-cm (1-inch) cubes

4 wooden or metal skewers

salt and pepper to taste

Prepare a marinade by mixing all the ingredients except for the pork cubes and salt and pepper.

Pour the marinade over the pork cubes and leave for 48 hours in the fridge.

Thread the pork on to the skewers and grill on a high heat for 4–5 minutes on each side, until all sides are brown. Sprinkle with salt and pepper and serve at once.

ATÚN
ANCHOA
BOLETUS CON JAMÓN
QUESO DE CABRA
PIQUILLO CON GAMBAS
PIQUILLO CON SOLOMILLO

LACÓN, ALCACHOFAS Y HABITAS
JAMÓN IBERICO, HABITAS Y SALMÓN
CECINA DE MORUCHA

MICHIRONES A LA MURCIANA
BROAD BEAN, HAM AND SAUSAGE STEW

This popular recipe originates in Murcia, Spain's smallest autonomous region, which lies between Valencia and Andalucía. It is similar to the Spicy broad bean and pork stew (see page 77), but the beef stock makes this a meatier dish.

(see page 77)

FOR 6 TAPAS

500g (1lb 2oz) dried broad beans, soaked for 48 hours

125g (4½oz) chorizo or other spicy sausage, cut in 1.25-cm (½-inch) slices

100g (3½oz) serrano ham, thickly cut and diced

1 ham bone

2 dried red chilli peppers, finely chopped

1.4 litres (2½ pints) beef stock

salt to taste

Place all the ingredients in a large saucepan – in the order in which they appear in the ingredients list – using just enough stock to cover. But don't add any salt and pepper yet.

Cover the pan and place over a high heat. When the mixture comes to the boil, turn the heat down and cook everything slowly for 1½–2 hours, or until the beans are tender. Top up the stock from time to time if necessary.

Remove the ham bone. Season with salt and pepper (adding salt before this stage would make the beans hard) and serve hot in individual earthenware dishes with chunks of French bread or a few bread sticks.

CHICKEN LEGS WITH PRUNES AND NUTS IN A BLACKBERRY SAUCE

Moorish influences sing in this luscious concoction of nuts, dried fruit, chicken (or poularde if you can get it) and sweet wine. Note that any dark dessert wine can be substituted for the Málaga variety.

FOR 12 TAPAS

75g (2¾oz) pine nuts

50g (1¾oz) walnuts, shelled and chopped

50g (1¾oz) unsalted pistachios, shelled and chopped

125g (4½oz) pitted prunes, chopped

12 organic chicken legs, boned

salt and pepper to taste

2 tbsp olive oil

200g (7oz) cloves garlic

2 small onions, sliced into half moons

2 potatoes, in 3mm (½ inch) slices

250ml (9fl oz) sweet Málaga wine

FOR THE BLACKBERRY SAUCE

125g (4¼oz) fresh or frozen blackberries

100g (3½oz) granulated sugar

2 tbsp balsamic vinegar

Mix the nuts and prunes together, then stuff the chicken legs with the mixture. Tie each leg together with kitchen string.

Place the stuffed legs on baking sheets, season, drizzle with olive oil, surround with garlic cloves, onions and potatoes, and bake in an oven preheated to 200°C (400° F) Gas mark 6 for 30–35 minutes, until the chicken is cooked.

Make the sauce by heating the berries and sugar with a few tbsp water, stirring to help the sugar dissolve in the berry juices. Add the vinegar, bring to the boil, then cook until syrupy – remember, it will thicken more as it cools. Set aside.

Warm the wine. Transfer the chicken legs, garlic and onions to a platter, pour the warmed wine over them and flambé immediately by touching the edge of the platter with the flame of a match. Serve the chicken accompanied by the sauce.

PATATAS CORTIJERAS CON PICADILLO DE CHORIZO

COUNTRY-STYLE POTATOES WITH CHORIZO AND PEPPERS

This recipe exploits abundant fresh Spanish vegetables, with the chorizo and ham acting as little more than seasoning. It's a perfect, sustaining mélange enveloped by lightly-cooked egg.

FOR 4 TAPAS

400g (14oz) potatoes, peeled and thinly sliced

50g (1¾oz) unsalted butter

3 tbsp olive oil for frying

125g (4½oz) onion, thinly sliced

20g (¾oz) red pepper, thinly sliced

20g (¾oz) green pepper, thinly sliced

3 cloves garlic, thinly sliced

30g (1oz) serrano ham, cut into thin strips

50g (1¾oz) chorizo, cut into 1-cm (½-inch) slices and lightly fried

2 eggs

salt and pepper to taste

Fry the potatoes in the butter and 2 tbsp of the oil over a low heat for 25 minutes, until the potatoes are tender. Remove the potatoes, leaving the fat behind, and put them in a bowl. Set aside.

In the same frying pan, sauté the onion and peppers over a low heat, adding more oil if you need it. When the vegetables are tender, add the garlic and cook until it is golden.

Add the vegetable mixture to the potatoes, stir in the meats and set aside.

Fry the eggs in a little oil until the white is firm. Add them to the vegetable and meat mixture and stir to break the eggs up. Combine all the ingredients. Season and tip on to a serving platter.

BOLITAS DE FLAMENQUÍN
FRIED PORK LOIN AND HAM BALLS

Quite simply delicious, this is an excellent tapa for large numbers of people, as the meatballs can be prepared in advance and served cold. The zing of the lemon juice makes all the difference. Delicious with sliced pan-fried potatoes and poached onion.

FOR 6 TAPAS

250g (9oz) pork loin, cut into thin slices lengthways

juice of 1 lemon

100g (3½oz) Iberian or serrano ham, cut into 6 slices

salt and pepper to taste

25g (1oz) flour

2 eggs, beaten

55g (2oz) dry breadcrumbs

olive oil for frying

Marinate the pork loin in the lemon juice for 1 hour.

Place a piece of ham on each pork slice, season, and roll up lengthwise to form cylinders.

Cut each cylinder into 2-cm (¾-inch) pieces, and squeeze into ball shapes.

Dip the balls in flour, then egg, then breadcrumbs and fry a few at a time in very hot oil, browning on all sides. Drain on paper towels and serve promptly.

LENTEJAS ESTOFADAS
LENTIL AND CHORIZO STEW

Well-blended, earthy flavours are the characteristics of this classic tapa, which is incredibly simple to prepare.

FOR 4 TAPAS

225g (8oz) green or brown lentils, soaked overnight

75ml (2½fl oz) virgin olive oil

1½ tsp Spanish paprika

1 small green pepper, diced

1 small onion, peeled and diced

1 small ripe tomato, peeled and diced

1 bay leaf

3 cloves garlic

100g (3½oz) chorizo or other spicy sausage, sliced

100g (3½oz) black pudding, sliced

1 small carrot, peeled and sliced

200g (7oz) potatoes, peeled and diced

Combine all the ingredients, except for the potatoes, in a heavy saucepan. Cover with cold water and bring to the boil. Reduce the heat and simmer for about 20 minutes.

Add the potatoes and continue to simmer for about 20 more minutes, until the potatoes and lentils are tender. Serve hot in individual soup bowls or dishes.

SALTEADO DE HÍGADO DE COCHINILLO CON SETAS Y PIÑONES

SAUTÉED PORK LIVER WITH MUSHROOMS AND PINE NUTS

At the long-established José Maria restaurant in Segovia, this dish is prepared with liver from a recently slaughtered suckling pig. It has quite a strong flavour so vary the quantity of mushrooms according to taste.

Sauté the pork liver in a little olive oil and set aside. Sauté the mushrooms and garlic in 2 tbsp olive oil until soft. Add the liver and heat through.

Create a mound of the liver and mushrooms on a serving plate, splash with the vinegar, garnish with the pine nuts and serve at once.

FOR 6 TAPAS

3 young pigs' livers, coarsely chopped

olive oil

200g (7oz) wild mushrooms, sliced

1 clove garlic, minced

1 tbsp white wine vinegar

2 tbsp pine nuts

HABAS CONDIMENTADAS

SPICY BROAD BEAN AND PORK STEW

Typical of southern Spanish 'peasant' food, this tapa contrasts the satisfying earthiness of pork and other meats with the mellow broad beans – a pulse that is undergoing a big revival.

FOR 6 TAPAS

500g (1lb 2oz) dried broad beans, soaked for 48 hours

30g (1¼oz) lomo Ibérico (cured pork loin)

30g (1¼oz) cured beef

50g (1¾oz) chorizo or other spicy sausage

10g (¼oz) smoked ham

1 small ham bone

125g (4½oz) chistorra or pork sausage

30g (1¼oz) fresh mint leaves

6 bay leaves

1 tsp cayenne pepper

1.4 litres (2½ pints) chicken stock or water

4 tbsp olive oil

25g (1oz) hot smoked Spanish paprika (*pimentón de la Vera*)

salt and pepper to taste

Place all the ingredients except the olive oil, paprika, salt and pepper, in a large saucepan – in the order in which they appear in the ingredients list – using just enough stock or water to cover the rest of the ingredients.

Heat the olive oil in a little frying pan, add the paprika and stir to blend. Pour this over the bean mixture, cover the pan and place over a high heat. When the mixture comes to the boil, turn the heat down and cook everything slowly for 1½–2 hours, or until the beans are tender. Top up the stock from time to time if necessary.

Remove the ham bone. Season the stew with salt and pepper (adding salt before this stage would make the beans hard) and serve hot in individual earthenware dishes.

MARISCOS Y PESCADOS

SEAFOOD

PAELLA DE BACALAO Y ESPINACAS

COD, SPINACH AND TOMATO PAELLA

Of the myriad forms of paella, this is one of the most delicious, with its distinctive flavour and dark colour. You can replace the salt cod with fresh cod or hake, but it is essential to use medium, round-grained rice. Aim for classic Calasparra rice: this absorbs masses of liquid therefore punches more flavour than other varieties.

FOR 6 TAPAS

150g (5½oz) salt cod

500g (1lb 2oz) fresh spinach, washed and destalked

4 tbsp olive oil

30g (1¼oz) pine nuts

250g (9oz) tomatoes, chopped

2 cloves garlic, crushed

2 tsp sweet paprika

1 dried chilli pepper, chopped

250g (9oz) Calasparra rice

500ml (18fl oz) vegetable stock

½ tsp saffron threads, infused in 2 tbsp just-boiled water for 15 minutes

salt to taste

lemon wedges to serve

Soak the salt cod in water for 48 hours, changing the water a couple of times a day. Rinse. Cut the flesh into strips, leaving any bones and the skin behind.

Cook the spinach, in the water left on the leaves after washing, in a covered pan over a medium heat for 4 minutes. Squeeze out the excess water and chop.

Heat the olive oil in a 60-cm (24-inch) paella pan or large frying pan. When very hot, add the cod, spinach, pine nuts, tomatoes, garlic, paprika and dried chilli. Lower the heat and cook, stirring constantly, for 6 minutes.

Add the rice and continue to cook, while stirring, for 2 more minutes. Add the stock and saffron. Season with salt and simmer for about 15 minutes, or until the stock has been absorbed and the rice is just cooked.

Remove from the heat, cover with a tea-towel, put the lid on, and allow to stand for 5 minutes. Garnish with lemon wedges and serve at once.

PINTXO DE SALMON AHUMADO CON BOQUERONES Y PIMIENTOS

SMOKED SALMON, ANCHOVY AND RED PEPPER TOASTS

Pintxo **get their name from the toothpick, or literally 'spike', that traditionally holds these delicious morsels together.**

FOR 4 TAPAS

- 4 anchovies marinated in vinegar (*boquerones*)
- 100g (3½oz) smoked salmon, cut into 4 slices and rolled into cylindrical shapes
- 1 red *piquillo* pepper (canned and drained), cut into 4 equal parts
- 4 wholegrain bread rounds, toasted

FOR THE VINAIGRETTE

- 1 spring onion, finely chopped
- 2 red *piquillo* peppers or 1 ordinary red pepper, seeded and finely chopped
- 1 hard-boiled egg, finely chopped
- ½ green pepper, seeded and finely chopped
- 200ml (7fl oz) extra virgin olive oil
- 5 tbsp white wine vinegar

To make the vinaigrette, combine the ingredients and mix well. Set aside.

To prepare the *pintxo*, place the anchovies skin-side-down, and put a roll of smoked salmon in the centre of each anchovy. Fold in half and top with a piece of red *piquillo* pepper.

Place each anchovy roll on top of a wholegrain toast and drizzle generously with vinaigrette.

BACALAO AHUMADO Y VINAGRETA DE TOMATE CON ACEITE DE ACEITUNA NEGRA

SMOKED COD, TOMATO AND BLACK OLIVE OIL TOASTS

There is a beguiling balance between the slightly sharp smoked cod and the earthy black olive oil in this recipe. A spoonful of French tapenade could easily be substituted for the olives in the oil. However don't skip the wholegrain bread – it's crucial to the balance.

FOR 8 TAPAS

8 slices or rounds wholegrain bread, toasted

100g (3½oz) smoked cod, thinly sliced

2 tbsp chopped chives or parsley

FOR THE VINAIGRETTE

1 large ripe tomato, peeled, pulp removed and finely chopped

5 tbsp extra virgin olive oil

1½ tbsp white wine vinegar

salt and pepper to taste

FOR THE BLACK OLIVE OIL

45g (1¾oz) pitted black olives, finely chopped

100ml (3½fl oz) extra virgin olive oil

Prepare the vinaigrette by mixing the tomato with the olive oil, white wine vinegar and seasoning.

Prepare the black olive oil by adding the chopped olives to the olive oil and blending together well.

Just before serving, place 8 toasts on a serving plate and moisten each with about 1 tsp black olive oil.

Put a slice of smoked cod on top of the toast and dress with a heaped tbsp of vinaigrette and a little more black olive oil. Garnish with chives or parsley.

ROLLITO DE CALABACÍN CON GAMBA Y BACON

FRIED COURGETTE, PRAWN AND BACON BUNDLES

This *pintxo* is quite fiddly to prepare, but once you have mastered the technique you will use it again and again.

Cut the courgette in half lengthways, then cut 4 × 3-mm (⅛-inch) slices, again lengthways, from one of the halves.

On each slice lay 1 strip of bacon and place 1 prawn on the end, then season with salt and pepper.

Roll the courgette up, being careful to ensure that the prawn stays in the centre, and secure with a toothpick.

Carefully dip the bundle in egg and then flour. Heat about 3cm (1¼ inches) olive oil in a frying pan and cook the rolls until golden. Drain on a paper towel.

Serve promptly on a sesame seed toast or cracker.

FOR 4 TAPAS

1 large courgette

4 strips lean bacon

4 prawns, cooked and peeled

salt and pepper to taste

1 beaten egg for coating

flour for coating

olive oil for frying

4 sesame seed toasts or crackers

ALMEJAS CON JAMÓN

CLAMS AND HAM IN CHILLI SAUCE

The classic Catalan combination of sea and mountain ingredients features in this favourite recipe. It is a simple but highly-flavoured dish that can easily be expanded to become a main course. Use mussels if you can't get hold of clams.

In a paellera or large frying pan, sauté the clams, ham and chilli pepper in hot oil until the clams begin to open.

Add the garlic, parsley, wine, salt and pepper, and continue to cook for about 2 more minutes. Discard any clams that have not opened. Spoon out into wide shallow bowls, pouring the sauce over last, and serve.

FOR 4 TAPAS

300g (10½oz) fresh clams, thoroughly cleaned (discard any that do not close)

60g (2¼oz) ham, cut in thin strips

1 medium red chilli pepper, seeded and finely chopped

2 tbsp olive oil for sautéing

2 cloves garlic, minced

2 tbsp finely chopped flat-leaf parsley

2 tbsp white wine

salt and pepper to taste

ANCHOA CON HUEVOS DE TRUCHA
ANCHOVY AND TROUT CAVIAR TOASTS

This classic recipe is a favourite among customers at Bar Txepetxa and is simple to make at home.

FOR 4 TAPAS

8 anchovy fillets marinated in vinegar
4 slices French bread, freshly toasted
4 tsp trout eggs

For each *pintxo,* lay 2 anchovy fillets on a slice of freshly toasted French bread.

Place 1 tsp trout eggs in a line down the middle of each toast. Serve immediately.

ANCHOA SALMÓN AHUMADO
ANCHOVY AND SMOKED SALMON TOASTS

A simple, subtle yet extravagant-tasting *pintxo*. Use the best smoked salmon you can find.

For each *pintxo,* lay 2 anchovy fillets on a slice of freshly toasted French bread.

Top each toast with a little mound of smoked salmon strips. Serve immediately.

FOR 4 TAPAS

8 anchovy fillets marinated in vinegar
4 slices French bread, freshly toasted
2 slices smoked salmon, cut into strips

ANCHOA JARDINERA
ANCHOVY AND VEGETABLE TOASTS

This deliciously fresh *pintxo* takes pride of place on a plate of mixed anchovy toasts, adding a splash of colour and a crisp texture.

Marinate the vegetables and herbs in the sunflower oil for half an hour to prevent them from drying out and to leave them glistening.

For each *pintxo*, lay 2 anchovy fillets on a slice of freshly toasted French bread. Spoon some of the marinated vegetables on top of the anchovies. Serve immediately.

FOR 4 TAPAS

1 small green pepper, finely chopped

1 small red pepper, finely chopped

1 small onion, finely chopped

2 cloves garlic, finely chopped

1 chilli pepper, halved, seeded and finely chopped

leaves from a small bunch of fresh parsley, finely chopped

3 tbsp sunflower oil

8 anchovy fillets marinated in vinegar

4 slices French bread, freshly toasted

LOMOS DE ANCHOA CON CREMA DE CENTOLLA
ANCHOVY AND CRAB TOASTS

A real taste of the sea! If you prefer a meatier flavour, add a slice of finely chopped cooked ham to the crab mixture.

Mix the crab, lettuce and egg together. Stir in the mayonnaise and lemon juice.

For each *pintxo*, lay 2 anchovy fillets on a slice of freshly toasted French bread, then cover with the crab mixture. Serve immediately.

FOR 4 TAPAS

meat of 1 cooked crab, finely chopped

2 lettuce leaves, finely shredded

1 hard-boiled egg, chopped

2 tbsp mayonnaise

2 tsp lemon juice

8 anchovy fillets marinated in vinegar

4 slices French bread, freshly toasted

LOMOS DE ANCHOA CON PÂTÉ DE OLIVAS

ANCHOVY, TAPENADE AND ONION TOASTS

An intensely flavoured *pintxo* – the one none of your guests will be able to forget. Delicious as an appetiser.

FOR 4 TAPAS

1 small onion, finely chopped

2 tbsp lemon juice

8 anchovy fillets marinated in vinegar

4 slices French bread, freshly toasted

3 tbsp tapenade

Marinate the onion in the lemon juice for at least 2 hours.

For each *pintxo*, put 2 anchovy fillets on a slice of freshly toasted French bread, cover with 2 tsp of tapenade, then sprinkle with the chopped onion. Serve immediately.

SUQUET DE PESCADO
CATALAN GRILLED FISH WITH BROTH

This Catalan classic goes well beyond the quantity boundaries of tapas, so it can move up your menu to slot in as a first or second course. It is excellent served with purées of aubergine and potatoes, which are both good for soaking up the ambrosial fish juices.

FOR 4 TAPAS

olive oil

2 cloves garlic, crushed

2 tbsp fresh chopped parsley

2 tomatoes, peeled, seeded and chopped

1 litre (1¾ pints) fish stock

4 medium-sized new potatoes, peeled and diced

½ tsp sweet Spanish paprika

salt and pepper to taste

4 × 175g (6oz) fish fillets, such as hake

In a little olive oil, sauté the garlic in a large frying pan until soft but not browned. Add the parsley and tomatoes and cook over a low heat, stirring, until the mixture thickens.

Add the fish stock, potatoes and paprika to the tomatoes and cook for about 10 minutes, or until the potatoes are cooked. Season the dish with salt and pepper.

While the broth is cooking, grill the fish fillets, skin-side down, until golden.

Serve the fish broth at once in bowls, with the fish fillets on the side.

TXALUPA

MUSHROOM, PRAWN AND CHEESE TARTLETS

Typically subtle in flavour, this *pintxo* also looks the part. Be sure to serve this with a refreshing white wine.

FOR 8 TAPAS

100g (3½oz) mushrooms, chopped

2 cloves garlic, finely minced

30g (1oz) butter

salt to taste

125ml (4fl oz) sparkling white wine

125ml (4fl oz) double cream

10 large prawns, peeled and chopped

125g (4½oz) *queso Ibérico* or mature Cheddar
  cheese, grated

FOR THE 8 TARTLET CASES

100g (3½oz) plain flour, plus extra for rolling

¼ tsp salt

40g (1½oz) butter, softened

1 small egg yolk

Make the pastry and prepare and cook the pastry cases according to the steps 1 and 2 of the recipe on page 93, omitting the pastry lids.

To make the filling, sauté the mushrooms and garlic in butter over a low heat for 20 minutes. Sprinkle on salt to taste, add the white wine, bring to the boil and reduce until there is barely any liquid left. Add the cream and prawns and continue to cook for 3 minutes, stirring occasionally. Remove from the heat.

Remove the pastry shells from their tins. Scoop the mixture into them and top with grated cheese. Place under the grill for 2 minutes, until the cheese is golden. Serve immediately.

HOJALDRE RELLENO
BLUE CHEESE AND ANCHOVY TARTLETS

Hidden between the pastry cases lies a rich, flavoursome filling, so be sure to serve this *pintxo* with a refreshing white wine. Txakoli, the Basque favourite, is ideal, but in its absence look for a light, dry sparkling white.

FOR 8 TAPAS

50g (1¾oz) Stilton or other soft blue cheese, crumbled

200ml (7fl oz) double cream, whipped

4 anchovy fillets in oil, drained and halved

FOR THE 8 TARTLET CASES

200g (7oz) plain flour, plus extra for rolling

½ tsp salt

90g (3¼oz) butter, softened

2 small egg yolks

To make the pastry, put the flour, salt and butter in a food processor and process with the pastry blade until the mixture resembles fine breadcrumbs. Add the egg yolks mixed with a bit of cold water a little at a time, continuing to blend. Just add enough to make the pastry come together in a ball. Wrap in cling-film and refrigerate for half an hour.

Roll the pastry out on a floured surface and cut it into shapes to fit 8 tartlet tins. Also cut out some 'lids'. Prick the bottoms of the tartlets and chill for 20 minutes. Fill the tartlets with a few dried beans so that they can bake blind. Put the lids on a baking sheet and cook both cases and lids in an oven pre-heated to 200°C (400°F) Gas mark 6 for about 15 minutes or until pale gold in colour. Cool in the tins.

For the filling, blend the cheese and the whipped cream with a wooden spoon until smooth. Set aside.

Remove the tartlet cases from their tins and place ½ an anchovy on the bottom of each one. Fill the pastry shells with the cheese and cream mixture and top with the pastry lid.

Place the pastries on a baking sheet and heat in a hot oven at 220°C (425°F) Gas mark 7 for 1 minute. Remove from the oven and serve.

QUESO, ANCHOA, PIMIENTO Y PUERRO SOBRE HOJALDRE

RED PEPPER, LEEK, ANCHOVY AND CREAM CHEESE TARTS

This two-bite size tapa is quick to make as well as to consume, yet the pastry case makes it satisfyingly filling. The quantity of anchovy or red pepper can be increased according to your taste.

FOR 4 TAPAS

1 leek, white portion only

4 anchovy fillets, drained of oil

½ small red pepper, roasted, peeled and cut into 4 equal strips

4 × 10cm (4 inch) squares of puff pastry, cooked

100g (3½oz) cream cheese

Cut the leek in half lengthways and cook it in boiling water until just soft. Drain and cut each half in half again lengthways.

Place 1 anchovy and 1 small strip of red pepper on each puff pastry square, then spread carefully with a quarter of the cream cheese. Top with a piece of the white leek.

Place under a grill for just long enough to heat through (about 3–4 minutes) and serve immediately.

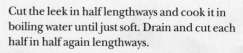

SARDINAS EN ESCABECHE

SARDINES MARINATED IN CHILLI, GARLIC AND BAY LEAVES

Simple, grilled sardines are ubiquitous throughout Spain, but here, the marinade transforms them into an aromatic sensation. While this tapa is explicitly garlicky, the slight bitterness of the bay leaves gives it a cutting edge. It tastes even better a day later.

FOR 6 TAPAS

12 fresh medium sardines, scaled and gutted

flour for coating

100ml (3½fl oz) olive oil

pepper to taste

1 dried red chilli pepper, minced

12 cloves garlic

1 tbsp sweet Spanish paprika

3 bay leaves

100ml (3½fl oz) white wine vinegar

100ml (3½fl oz) dry white wine

100ml (3½fl oz) water

salt to taste

At least 2½ hours before serving, coat the sardines lightly with flour on both sides and quickly fry in hot oil to brown each side. Place in a shallow earthenware dish.

Strain the oil that was used to fry the sardines and, when cool, return it to the frying pan and add the pepper, chilli pepper and garlic. Fry gently until the garlic is golden.

Remove from the heat and add the paprika, bay leaves, vinegar, wine, water and salt to the pan. Bring to the boil and boil for 1 minute.

Pour the hot liquid over the sardines and leave to marinate at room temperature for at least 2 hours.

These sardines can be served hot, cold or at room temperature.

MEJILLONES EN SALSA PICANTE
MUSSELS IN SPICY SAUCE

It is essential to leave the grilling of this recipe until just before you serve it – that way it tastes fresh and hot. Find mussels that are as plump, juicy and fresh as possible and choose cheese such as a mature Cheddar, with a sharp, tangy flavour.

FOR 4 TAPAS

4 bay leaves

salt and pepper to taste

1kg (2¼lb) mussels, scrubbed, (discard any that remain open)

50ml (2fl oz) olive oil

1 large onion, chopped

6 cloves garlic, minced

½ red chilli pepper, seeded and finely chopped

1 tsp flour

1½ tsp hot smoked Spanish paprika (*pimentón de la Vera*)

100g (3½oz) Cebreiro cheese, or similar sharp cheese that melts well, grated

In a deep, heavy pan, bring about 100ml (3½fl oz) water, with 2 bay leaves and a pinch of salt, to the boil. Add the mussels, cover the pan and cook for about 4–5 minutes, until the shells open.

Remove the mussels from the pan, discard any that haven't opened, then remove the lids from the rest and throw the empty shells away. Place the mussels in their half-shells in a shallow oven-proof dish, pour the cooking liquid over them and set them aside.

Heat the oil in a large frying pan. Add the onion, garlic, chilli and the other 2 bay leaves. Sauté gently over a low heat until the onion turns golden.

Stir in the flour and paprika and cook for 1 minute, stirring constantly.

Take the pan off the heat and slowly add the mussel cooking liquid, stirring all the time to incorporate it well. Put the pan back on the heat and cook until the sauce thickens. Remove from the heat and mix in a blender to achieve a smooth sauce.

Return the sauce to the pan, add the mussels and cook for 3–4 minutes to warm through. Arrange the mussels and sauce in a serving bowl, sprinkle with grated cheese, and put under a medium grill until the cheese has melted. Serve immediately.

BONITO EN SASHIMI MARINADO

MARINATED TUNA CUBES

Carlos Abellán serves this tapa in a porcelain dish specially designed for such cubes, but the food's so stylish it would look good on almost anything. Make sure the tuna is ultra-fresh, as this is the heart of the dish. For an even more intense flavour, lightly sprinkle some powdered ginger or some grated fresh ginger over the cubes.

FOR 4 TAPAS

- - - - - - - - - - - - -

50ml (2fl oz) soy sauce

50ml (2fl oz) sunflower oil

150g (5½oz) fresh tuna, cut into
   3-cm (1¼-inch) cubes

2 tbsp sesame seeds

soy oil

Prepare the marinade by mixing the soy sauce and sunflower oil together. Add the tuna and leave it to marinate for at least 12 hours.

Thread the tuna cubes on skewers. Top each cube with a sprinkling of sesame seeds and drizzle with a little soy oil. Serve promptly.

VENTRESCA DE ATÚN CONFITADA CON ARROZ A LA CRÈME DE GINGEMBRE

BAKED TUNA SERVED WITH GINGERED RICE

The tender fresh fish and sweet red onion are perfectly complemented by the delicate ginger flavour of the rice. It is essential to respect the baking time in order to preserve the flaky texture and colour of the tuna. The dish looks wonderful on a large platter or served in small, flat bowls. If the ingredients are multiplied, this tapa can equally well be served as a main course.

FOR 4 TAPAS

15g (½oz) butter

½ tsp finely chopped fresh ginger

50g (1¾oz) long-grain rice

3 tbsp double cream

2 tbsp finely chopped parsley plus

   1 tbsp for garnish

salt and white pepper to taste

250g (9oz) belly of tuna, skinned and filleted

2 tbsp finely chopped red onion

extra virgin olive oil

Melt the butter in a saucepan and sauté the ginger for about a minute. Add the rice, stir it around in the butter and ginger, and add 100ml (3½fl oz) water. Bring to the boil, turn the heat down low, cover and cook for about 15 minutes. The rice should be tender, but not totally soft, and the water should have evaporated. Stir in the cream, parsley, salt and pepper. Keep warm.

Preheat the oven to 170°C (325°F) Gas mark 3. Cut the tuna into four equal parts, then arrange it in a single layer in a lightly oiled oven-proof dish. Cover tightly with aluminium foil and place in the oven. Cook for 8 minutes.

Remove from the oven, salt lightly, and transfer to a serving plate. Arrange the pieces in a ring, leaving space in the centre for the rice. Sprinkle each piece of tuna with chopped onion and the remaining parsley. Finally, drizzle with extra virgin olive oil.

Spoon the creamy gingered rice into the centre of the plate and then serve immediately.

ANCHOA CON QUESO

ANCHOVY WITH SHEEP'S CHEESE ON TOAST

A wonderfully salty tapa – the sheep's cheese and anchovy combine to create a powerful flavour.

Lightly toast the slices of French bread on each side until golden.

Lay a slice of sheep's cheese on each toast, and then top with an anchovy fillet.

FOR 4 TAPAS

4 slices French bread
4 slices sheep's cheese
4 anchovy fillets

LOMO IBÉRICO DE BELLOTA, KAVIAR O SALMÓN AHUMADO

ORGANIC CURED BEEF, CAVIAR OR SMOKED SALMON ON TOAST

These *pintxos* from José Luis are more ideas than recipes, but they make luxuriously simple snacks and look great on a plate together topped with mayonnaise.

Lightly toast the slices of French bread on each side until golden.

Lay slices of the best quality cured beef on four toasts, a heaped spoonful of lumpfish roe on a further four and a slice of smoked salmon on the final four.

FOR 12 TAPAS

12 slices French bread
4 slices cured beef
120g (4oz) lumpfish roe
4 slices smoked salmon

TARTAR DE AHUMADOS
SMOKED FISH TARTARE

A delicious combination of three smoked fish, this is another salty tapa that makes a fabulous appetiser. The onion and capers add a piquancy that will really get your juices flowing.

Lightly toast the French bread on each side.

Mix the smoked anchovies, salmon and trout together. Add the diced onion and capers and mayonnaise.

Heap a large spoonful of the paste on to each slice of toast.

FOR 4 TAPAS

50g (1¾oz) smoked anchovies, finely chopped

50g (1¾oz) smoked salmon, finely chopped

50g (1¾oz) smoked trout, finely chopped

2 tsp diced onion

2 tsp diced capers

75g (2¾oz) mayonnaise

4 slices French bread

SARDE EN SAOR
MARINATED SARDINES
WITH ONIONS IN SHERRY

Michele Gallana of Valencia learnt this traditional Venetian seamen's way of marinating sardines from his grandmother. To give it a Valencian touch, mix in a handful of pine nuts and raisins just before serving.

Coat the sardines with flour and fry them in a thin layer of hot oil until they are delicately browned on both sides. Drain on paper towels.

In a separate pan, slowly fry the onions in oil until they are golden. Remove from the heat, add the vinegar and seasoning and stir well.

Alternate layers of sardines and onions in a deep dish, beginning with sardines and ending with the onions. Cool and refrigerate for at least 2 hours.

To serve, spoon generous portions on to individual plates.

FOR 6 TAPAS

500g (1lb 2oz) small fresh sardines, gutted and scaled

flour for coating

olive oil for frying

4 onions, finely chopped

125ml (4fl oz) white wine vinegar

salt and pepper to taste

MEJILLONES À LA MARINERA
FISHERMEN'S MUSSELS

Choose large, plump mussels to complement the generous tomato sauce, with its aromatic echoes of the Mediterranean.

FOR 6 TAPAS

- 750g (1lb 10oz) fresh mussels, scrubbed, any that remain open discarded
- 75ml (2½fl oz) dry white wine
- 1 bay leaf
- 2 tbsp olive oil
- 1 large onion, finely chopped
- 1 red pepper, finely chopped
- 1 green pepper, finely chopped
- 2 cloves garlic, minced
- 2 ripe tomatoes, finely chopped
- ⅛ tsp cayenne pepper
- white pepper to taste

Place the mussels in a large pot with the wine and bay leaf and cook, covered, over a high heat for a few minutes, shaking occasionally until the shells open. Remove to a serving platter, discarding any mussels whose shells have not opened, and keep warm. Reserve the cooking liquid.

Heat the olive oil in a saucepan. Sauté the onion, peppers and garlic until softened. Add the tomatoes and cayenne pepper and cook for about 15 minutes, until the mixture is thick. Stir in a little of the cooking liquid from the mussels and season with white pepper.

Pour the sauce over the mussels and serve at once.

ESCALIBADA CON CABALLA EN ESCABECHE

MARINATED MACKEREL
WITH ROASTED VEGETABLES

Escalibada is an eastern Spanish classic that makes full use of the abundant fresh vegetables grown locally. The name comes from the Catalan word for 'charred', and ideally the vegetables should be cooked over a barbecue to get a really full, smoky flavour. *Escalibada* can be served with any kind of preserved or marinated fish, though mackerel work perfectly.

FOR 6 TAPAS

1 aubergine, halved lengthways

1 courgette, halved lengthways

1 onion, peeled and quartered

1 red pepper, halved and seeded

1 fennel bulb, trimmed, quartered and central heart removed

olive oil for roasting

ground rock salt to taste

100ml (3½fl oz) dry white wine

200ml (7fl oz) olive oil

4 mackerel fillets, cleaned and prepared

6 cloves

4 cloves garlic, unpeeled

4 bay leaves

Place the vegetables (except for the garlic) cut-side-down on a baking sheet, brush with olive oil, season with rock salt and roast at 200°C (400°F) Gas mark 6 for 35 minutes.

To prepare the marinade, whisk together the wine and olive oil. Put the mackerel fillets in a wide saucepan and pour over just enough marinade to cover them. Add the cloves, garlic and bay, cover the saucepan, and simmer for 15 minutes.

Peel the skin from the roast pepper halves and cut the stem off the aubergine halves. Slice the vegetables thinly and arrange in the centre of a plate. Place the mackerel fillets on top of the vegetables and garnish the rim of the plate with the bay leaves and garlic cloves. This tapa can be served warm or cool, but not refrigerated.

FIDEOS A LA MARINERA
SEAFOOD PASTA

Although fiddly to prepare, this tapa looks and tastes stunning and you may want to increase the quantities to make it into a main dish.

FOR 6 TAPAS

- - - - - - - - - - - -

1 medium onion, diced

2 medium green peppers, diced

2 tomatoes, diced

2 cloves garlic, minced

olive oil for frying

75ml (2½fl oz) white wine

1 litre (1¾ pints) water

¼ tsp saffron threads, infused in just a little boiled water

250g (9oz) clams, scrubbed and washed and any that will not close discarded

150g (5½oz) cuttlefish, cleaned, prepared and cut into small strips

150g (5½oz) prawns, peeled

100g (3½oz) hake, filleted and cut into small pieces

salt and pepper to taste

200g (7oz) short lengths of spaghetti or a pasta shape such as *tubetti lunghi*

chopped parsley, to garnish

In a heavy-bottomed sauté pan, fry the onion, peppers, tomatoes and garlic in olive oil until soft.

Add the white wine and cook for about 10 minutes to reduce the liquid.

Add the water and saffron liquid and cook on a high heat for 15 minutes.

Add the clams, cuttlefish, prawns, hake, seasoning and pasta and continue to cook over a low heat for about 10 minutes, until the fish and pasta are tender and the liquid has been absorbed. Discard any clams that have not opened. Serve in individual earthenware dishes decorated with chopped parsley sprigs.

PUDIN DE ESPINACAS

SPINACH PRAWN LOAF

This cold, mousse-like tapa is ideal for hot weather, when appetites are not too big. It makes the perfect accompaniment for a glass of beer or sangrìa in the summer.

FOR 4 TAPAS

400g (14oz) spinach, washed and destalked

1 medium onion, finely chopped

2 medium tomatoes, finely chopped

2 tbsp olive oil

100g (3½oz) raw prawns, peeled

salt and pepper to taste

125ml (4fl oz) milk

125ml (4fl oz) double cream

4 eggs

Cook the spinach in the water that clings to the leaves after washing, in a covered saucepan over a medium heat for about 4 minutes. Drain and wring the excess water out by pressing the cooked leaves between two dinner plates – the spinach must be very dry. Set aside.

Sauté the onion and tomatoes in the olive oil until softened. Turn the heat up to make some of the liquid evaporates. Add the spinach and prawns, season and stir. Cook over a low heat for a few minutes, then cool.

Put the prawn and spinach mixture into a blender and add the milk, cream and eggs. Whirl until smooth and creamy. Test for seasoning and season to taste.

Pour the mixture into a lightly oiled loaf tin and bake in a bain-marie at 180°C (350°F) Gas mark 4 for about 45 minutes, until firm. To test if the loaf is cooked, insert a skewer into the centre – it should come out clean. Cool, then refrigerate for at least 2 hours.

To serve, unmould and cut into slices of desired thickness. Serve with a seasonal salad garnish of your choice.

PURRUSALDA
POTATO AND COD STEW

The classic marriage of cod and potatoes has been developed into a hearty, appetising tapa, lifted by Mediterranean tomatoes and olive oil.

FOR 4 TAPAS

250g (9oz) salt cod

4 leeks, cleaned and coarsely chopped

4 tbsp olive oil

1kg (2¼lb) potatoes, peeled and diced

1¼ litres (1¾ pints) fish stock

3 ripe tomatoes, chopped

salt and pepper to taste

Soak the salt cod in water for 48 hours, changing the water a couple of times a day. Rinse. Flake the flesh, leaving any bones and the skin behind.

In a large pan, sauté the leeks in the olive oil until tender. Add the potatoes and continue to sauté over a very low heat for 15 more minutes.

Add the fish stock and tomatoes, bring to the boil, and simmer for 20 minutes.

Add the flaked salt cod and simmer for 10 more minutes. Season to taste, and serve hot in individual soup bowls.

PUDIN DE ESPÁRRAGOS VERDES Y GAMBAS
ASPARAGUS AND PRAWN FLANS

The Spanish word 'pudin', an aborted version of the English 'pudding', is used to describe a savoury tapa that resembles a French mousse. This version has a pleasingly rough texture and undemanding flavours.

FOR 4 TAPAS

½ medium onion, finely chopped

olive oil

100g (3½oz) prawns, peeled and chopped

100g (3½oz) green asparagus, preferably wild, cut into small pieces

50ml (2fl oz) dry sherry

225ml (8fl oz) whipping cream

3 eggs, beaten

salt and white pepper to taste

mayonnaise to serve

A day before serving, sauté the onion in a little olive oil until it is soft.

Add the prawns, asparagus and sherry and cook over a low heat until the liquid has almost disappeared.

Add the whipping cream, beaten eggs and a little salt and pepper and mix well.

Pour into lightly oiled individual daniole moulds. Set these in a bain-marie and bake in an oven pre-heated to 180°C (350°F) Gas mark 4 for 35 minutes. Remove from the oven, cool and then refrigerate for 12 hours.

Just before serving, turn the flans out, place on individual plates, and top each one with a dollop of mayonnaise.

ENSALADA DE BACALAO CON

SALT COD AND ORANGE SALAD

This ultra-simple tapa offers a refreshing combination of flavours, but it is essential to use good quality salt cod and luscious oranges. If you have individual moulds, so much the better, as cutting slices of this salad tends to make it crumble.

FOR 4 TAPAS

800g (1¾lb) salt cod

300g (10½oz) juicy orange segments, skin and pips removed, diced

2 tbsp snipped chives

4 black olives

extra virgin olive oil to taste

Soak the salt cod in water for 48 hours, changing the water a couple of times a day. Remove the flesh, discard the skin and bones, and flake the flesh.

Mix the orange flesh with the chives, then divide the mixture into individual moulds. Top with the flaked salt cod and compress well.

Refrigerate for at least 1 hour before turning out on to plates to serve.

Decorate each portion with a black olive and drizzle with olive oil.

PIMIENTOS DEL PIQUILLO RELLENOS

DEEP-FRIED RED PIQUILLO PEPPERS WITH A TUNA STUFFING

Although *piquillo* peppers are grown in Navarra and Rioja, they are in demand throughout the peninsula for their concentrated juiciness, sweetness and velvety texture. If you can't find fresh ones, use the tinned variety.

FOR 4 TAPAS

8 whole red *piquillo* peppers, fresh or canned, or 4 ordinary red peppers

50g (1oz) butter

1 tbsp sunflower oil

30g (1oz) plain flour

10g (¼oz) cornflour

300ml (½ pint) milk

salt and pepper to taste

freshly grated nutmeg to taste

150g (5½oz) tinned tuna in oil, drained and flaked

beaten egg for coating

flour for coating

olive or sunflower oil for frying

If you are using fresh peppers rather than tinned, halve and seed them and then grill them until blistered and black in places. Cool and then peel off the skins.

To prepare the stuffing, make a white sauce by melting the butter in a pan with the oil. Add the flour and cornflour, stirring constantly until the flours and fats have come together and you have a roux. Cook until the roux is pale gold in colour, then remove from the heat. Add the milk, a little at a time, making sure each addition is incorporated into the roux before you add the next bit. Put the pan back on the heat and bring to the boil, stirring continuously to obtain a smooth sauce. Cook over a low heat, stirring from time to time, for 5 minutes.

Take the sauce off the heat and season well with salt, pepper and nutmeg. Add the tuna, mix, and then allow to cool. Refrigerate for 12 hours.

About half an hour before serving, fill the peppers with the tuna mixture, taking care not to tear them. Fold the peppers over the filling. Dip them in the egg and then flour and carefully lower them into about 10cm (4 inches) hot oil. Fry until lightly browned on allsides. Drain them on paper towels and serve immediately.

CALAMARES PICA-PICA

SQUID IN A TOMATO, GARLIC AND RED WINE SAUCE

Easy to make yet oozing with flavour, this Mallorcan tapa is a real hit in Valencia. Make sure the squid you use is small and tender.

FOR 4 TAPAS

- - - - - - - - - - - - -

100ml (3½fl oz) olive oil

500g (1lb 2oz) squid, cleaned, prepared and cut into 5-cm (2-inch) pieces

1 onion, coarsely chopped

200g (7oz) tomatoes, coarsely chopped

2 cloves garlic, crushed

1 red pepper, seeded and chopped

1 bay leaf

200ml (7fl oz) red wine

100ml (3½fl oz) fish stock

chives, to serve

Heat the olive oil in a large saucepan. Add the squid and stir-fry for 1 minute. Add the onion and tomatoes and fry for 5 more minutes.

Add the garlic, pepper, bay leaf, red wine and stock, stir and then simmer for 20 minutes. Serve hot in earthenware dishes, with crusty bread and chive stalks laid across.

CHEFS

Carles Abellán, Barcelona
With his elegant restaurant and tapas bar, Comerç24, Carles flung open the doors of fame. Then followed funky Tapaç²⁴, then El Velódromo. Ferran Adriá being a past mentor, the food is fun, imaginative yet rooted in Catalunya.
— Catalan grilled fish with broth 91
— Marinated tuna cubes 100

Bar Pinotxo, Barcelona
The Bayen family, commanded by bow-tied Juanito, runs the renowned little Bar Pinotxo inside the thronging Boquería market. Le tout Barcelona has sat on a stool here to sample their flavoursome, freshly cooked Catalan tapas.
— Chickpeas with black pudding in garlic and parsley 47
— Sardines marinated in chilli, garlic and bay leaves 97

Enrique Becerra & Diego Ruiz, Seville
Backed by five generations of his family in the restaurant business, Enrique Becerra's unrivalled knowledge of Sevillian food has put classics such as these on the menu of his acclaimed restaurant.
— Asparagus and prawn flans 115
— Lentil and chorizo stew 74
— Minted lamb meatballs 59

Luis Benavente, Madrid
Luis ran Bocaito, a charmingly old-fashioned bar-restaurant in central Madrid, until a few years ago. Some of his original tapas just never went away.
— Young garlic, broad bean and ham omelette 35

Patxi Bergara & Blanca Ameztoy, San Sebastián
Bar Bergara, steered by this industrious husband-and-wife team, is an institution in the Gros district, making high quality, award-winning pintxos.
— Blue cheese and anchovy tartlets 93
— Mushroom, prawn & cheese tartlets 92

Bodegas Campos, Córdoba
A series of chefs at the illustrious Bodegas Campos, a spectacular, rambling hacienda open since 1908, follow house tapas recipes that incorporate the best of Andalucian produce.
— Country-style potatoes with chorizo and peppers 70
— Fried pork loin and ham balls 73
— Frittata of garden vegetables 21

Rosas María Borja & Isabel Capote Domínguez, Seville
Borja and Domínguez, two brilliant, creative chefs, launched these tapas at one of Seville's most hip (and packed) bars, La Eslava.
— Honey-baked chicken thighs 43
— Potato and cod stew 114
— Spinach prawn loaf 112

Joaquín Campos, Madrid
Dynamic Joaquin has now jumped ship to live in Shanghai, taking tapas to the Chinese. He devised these dishes for a tapas bar in Madrid, although he originates from Malaga.
— Baked tuna served with ginger rice 101
— Fried goat's cheese with honey 36
— Iberian ham and broad bean salad 44

Michele Gallana, Valencia
When he ran the trailblazing Santa Companya wine bar, Michele, who hails from Venice in Italy, infused new gastronomic ideas into Valencia's offerings.
— Cheese and quince 39
— Marinated sardines with onions in sherry 105
— Spicy steak tartare 62

Emiliano García Domene, Valencia
Emiliano has owned the illustrious Bodega Montaña in Valencia's old fishing quarter for over 20 years, introducing wines from all over the world to accompany ambrosial tapas.

— Artichoke hearts with black olive oil 12
— Deep-fried red piquillo peppers with tuna stuffing 119
— Spicy broad bean and pork stew 77

Lola Gracía Burgos & Emiliano Sánchez Pincón, Seville
Lola, wife of the owner of Bar Giralda, together with chef Emiliano devise recipes for their constantly changing menu.
— Potatoes of great importance 20

Paco Guzmán, Barcelona
Guzmán, the impassioned chef-owner of fashionable restaurants Santa María and Santa, conjures up delectable fusion dishes derived from his experience working in France and Asia.
— Duck's liver with sweet pears and Szechuan pepper 48
— Pumpkin, chestnut, feta cheese and pomegranate salad 14

Josep Manubens, Barcelona
The Cal Pep bar is a Barcelona legend, prompting snaking queues of eager customers from all over the world. The reason for this is the astute yet creative tapas created by chef-owner Josep ('Pep'), all of which are cooked and served at the packed bar with fantastic aplomb.
— Clams and ham in chilli sauce 86
— Tricky tortilla 29

Mari-Carmen Manuel & Josecho Marañón, San Sebastián
In the web of highly competitive pintxo bars in San Sebastián old town, right by the harbour, the Marañón family's Bar Txepetxa monopolises the anchovy market.
— Anchovy and crab toasts 89
— Anchovy and smoked salmon toasts 88
— Anchovy and trout caviar toasts 88
— Anchovy and vegetable toasts 89

— *Anchovy, tapenade and onion toasts* 90

— *Red pepper, leek, anchovy and cream cheese tarts* 94

— *Red peppers stuffed with black pudding* 53

Carlos Martinez & Meay Espinosa, Logroño
The capital of the Rioja wine region boasts an unrivalled concentration of bars in just one street, Calle Laurel. Casa Pali is one of these and serves simple tapas classics such as these.
— *Fried asparagus, ham and cheese bundles* 52
— *Aubergine and cheese fritters* 31
— *Ham croquettes* 55

José Luis Ruiz Solaguren, Madrid
José Luis, originally Basque and now in his eighties, is Madrid's king of tapas. Owning no fewer than 10 taverns and two restaurants, he is responsible for raising pintxos to a higher level in the capital.
— *Anchovy with sheep's cheese on toast* 103
— *Organic cured beef, caviar or smoked salmon on toast* 103
— *Smoked fish tartare* 104

Colin Ward, Valencia
A Londoner who grew up in Andalucia, Colin Ward first came to Valencia with a rock n' roll band. As a cook, he excelled at the city's Mediterranean classics as well as recipes from his Mallorcan wife.
— *Cod, spinach and tomato paella* 80
— *Marinated mackerel with roasted vegetables* 109
— *Squid in a tomato, garlic and red wine sauce* 121

Esteban Miñana, Valencia
La Bodeguilla del Gato is among Valencia's favourite nocturnal haunts in groovy El Carmen, serving Esteban's tasty tapas.
— *Fishermen's mussels* 106
— *Spicy sausage in red wine* 60
— *Squid in a tomato, garlic and red wine sauce* 121

José María Ruiz, Segovia
King Juan Carlos himself has frequented José Maria's landmark restaurant, which remains totally dedicated to the produce of Castile, including such delicacies as suckling pig.
— *Leeks with a summer vegetable vinaigrette* 15
— *Sautéed pork liver with mushrooms and pine nuts* 76
— *Traditional Segovian pork and potato 'fry-up'* 51

Lourdes Ybarra, Seville
While working as head cook at the ever-popular Bar Europa in Sevilla, Lourdes helped to establish these typical Andaluz dishes on the city's legendary tapas map.
— *Chilled almond soup* 32
— *Ratatouille with quail's egg* 24
— *Salt cod and orange salad* 116

María Agustina Ostiz, Pamplona
María Agustina, who trained under Juan Marí Arzak, devised these pintxo recipes while working at Pamplona's award-winning bar and restaurant, Baserri.
— *Fried courgette, prawn and bacon bundles* 85
— *Smoked cod, tomato and black olive oil toasts* 84
— *Smoked salmon, anchovy and red pepper toast* 83

Raquel Sabater, Alicante
Granddaughter of the founder of one of Alicante's oldest tapas bars, Mesón de Labradores, Raquel loves old-style tapas such as these.
— *Broad bean, ham and sausage stew* 66
— *Poor man's potatoes* 16
— *Spicy pork kebabs* 63

Manuel Zamora, Seville
Using local ingredients, this ebullient, self-taught cook brought great fantasy to Seville's Bodeguita Casablanca, known as a temple for discerning tapas-hunters.
— *Andalucian-style spinach with chickpeas* 17
— *Chicken legs with prunes and nuts in a blackberry sauce* 69
— *Potato tortilla with whisky sauce* 28
— *Seasoned potato mash* 18
— *Seafood pasta* 111

Miguel Reguera García, Salamanca
When Miguel opened Momo, it took Salamanca by storm, bringing designer pintxos to a conservative, essentially Renaissance town.
— *Cream cheese and leek toasts* 32
— *Foie gras, courgette and bitter orange toasts* 42
— *Ham, artichoke, broad bean and alioli toasts* 56
— *Ham, broad bean, smoked salmon and alioli toasts* 57

José Angel Valladeres, Paloma Tatay, Andrés Goméz & Fernando Estrada, Madrid
In 1995 four friends took over a peeling tavern, named it Astur and set about introducing Spain's rural delicacies to local palates. The formula worked and these recipes show why.
— *Lamb stew* 58
— *Mushrooms in parsley sauce* 25
— *Mussels in spicy sauce* 98

INDEX

ACKNOWLEDGEMENTS

I would like to thank the chefs
and bar-owners featured in
this book for responding so
positively to my requests,
collaborating with such
good humour and feeding
my stomach and soul so
magnificently. I am also grateful
to the following for their help
and advice: Francoçe Butscher
at Turmadrid; José Ferri at the
Valencia Region Tourist Board;
the San Sebastián Convention
Bureau; María José Sevilla at the
Spanish Embassy, London; Pilar
Faro; Mar Mateo; Christopher
Branton; Tamsyn Hill; Tim
O'Grady; Lorna Scott-Fox and,
not least, our recipe translator,
Ana Sims, who succeeded
with humour in the face of
sometimes daunting odds.
I would also like to stress my
gratitude to the photographer,
Jan Baldwin, who sailed
through the shoots with
immense serenity and humour
Thanks also to Diane Henry
for her recipe-testing, to
Becca Spry who originally
commissioned this book, to
Alison Starling for reviving
it and to Jo Wilson for
seeing through this new
revised version.

GLOSSARY

In collecting these recipes from my favorite tapas chefs in Spain, I selected those with ingredients that were easily available beyond the Iberian frontiers. However, even these sometimes need explaining – as do some tapas terms – so use the following glossary to identify exactly what they are.

aceite de oliva: a blend of refined and virgin olive oils with far less flavour than virgin olive oil. The basic olive oil for frying.

aceite de oliva virgen: virgin olive oil with acidity levels up to 4 per cent, quite mild in flavour.

aceite de oliva virgen extra (*primera presión*): extra virgin olive oil (first cold pressing) with an acidity level below 1 per cent and a distinctive flavour. Ideal for dressings and drizzlings.

alioli: similar to mayonnaise, theoretically without the egg yolk, this Catalan sauce is made from garlic, salt, oil and optional lemon juice. It is, however, hard to make without the egg yolk.

anchoas: fresh anchovies, salted anchovy fillets or fillets in oil.

bacalao: confusingly, the Spanish word refers both to fresh cod and, far more commonly, to salt cod. The latter form is omnipresent throughout the peninsula and comes in numerous qualities, dependent on origin.

boquerones: anchovies that are pickled in a wine vinegar.

butifarra: mildly peppered Catalan pork sausage, white or black in colour, sometimes including breadcrumbs and with a finer texture than morcilla.

cecina: cured beef, typical of León in Old Castile, where it is salted, smoked and cured. Originally made from horsemeat, it is served very finely sliced.

chorizo: spicy cooked sausage flavoured with paprika, salt, pepper and garlic. It comes in fresh, smoked or cured versions. The best is 95 per cent pork.

embutidos: a generic term for sausage meats, whether cured, cooked or fresh.

escabeche: pickling brine or marinade, usually made of oil, vinegar, peppercorns, bay leaf, and/or spices.

guindilla: the chilli pepper, which is a New World import to Spain, plays a major role in Spanish cooking. Larger ones are generally milder than smaller ones and the hottest are the dried variety. Red chillies (ripened green chillies) have a sweeter flavour.

jamón ibérico: cured ham from Iberian black-coated pigs.

jamón ibérico de bellota: Spain's top cured ham from black-coated pigs fed on acorns in the wild.

jamón serrano: mass-produced cured ham, still delicious and often used in cooked dishes, when it is more thickly sliced.

jamón de York: cooked ham

morcilla: the Spanish version of black pudding (made from pig's blood), which may contain pine nuts and/or rice. The best is from Burgos in Old Castile.

Pedro Ximénez: a very sweet sherry often used in cooking.

pil-pil: a garlic and olive oil sauce that is sometimes made green by the addition of parsley (*salsa verde*).

pimentón (paprika): the Spanish have two types: *pimentón de la vera* (from Extremadura), a smoked paprika that comes in hot, sweet and sweet-sour varieties; and straightforward *pimentón*, sun-dried paprika, also in hot and sweet versions and made in Murcia.

pimientos del piquillo: small red peppers, oozing with sweetness and flavour, that are often used in their canned incarnation as they are only grown in Navarra.

pintxo: canapé-style tapas, originally from the Basque region.

pisto: originally from La Mancha, this is a more condensed, Iberian version of ratatouille made from fried peppers, onion, tomato, garlic, courgette and aubergine.

raciones: slightly larger portions than tapas.

requesón: a fresh curd cheese that is similar to Italian ricotta or cottage cheese.

ventresca de atún/bonito: the belly of the tuna fish, regarded as the most tender part and therefore the most sought-after. Also to be found in canned versions at speciality grocers.

vinagre: Spaniards only use wine or sherry vinegar, usually red.